FOLENS HISTORY

HL

CW01637279

BACK TO THE PAST

CONTENTS

Unit	*Theme*	*Page*
1.	WHAT IS HISTORY?	2
2.	TIME AND CHRONOLOGY	4
3.	PERIODS AND CENTURIES	6
4.	HOW DO WE KNOW?	8
5.	ASKING HISTORICAL QUESTIONS	10
6.	FINDING OUT FROM PICTURES	12
7.	USING WRITTEN EVIDENCE	14
8.	LEARNING FROM ARTEFACTS	16
9.	TALKING WITH PEOPLE	18
10.	LOOKING AT MAPS	20
11.	BUILDINGS AS EVIDENCE	22
12.	PROBLEMS OF EVIDENCE	24
13.	THE CONCEPTS OF HISTORY	26
14.	ORGANISATION/PRESENTATION	30
	Acknowledgements	32

CAROLE BROWN

1. WHAT IS HISTORY?

Target

* To understand what we mean by history.

Have you ever wondered what it was like to live one hundred years ago when your great, great grandparents were children? What did they do, think and feel? What events happened during their lives? Why might they have acted in certain ways?

Written in pencil on the back of this photograph is 'Carole and Malcolm, 6th March, 1965'.

? *What is happening in this photograph?*

? *How do you think the people are feeling?*

History is about discovering answers to these and many more questions by making a journey of adventure into the past.

Before going on any journey you need to decide what to take with you. This book is rather like your suitcase. It helps you to learn all the skills you will need to find out about the people and events of the past.

The book will also introduce you to some of the concepts or ideas of history and provides the evidence for you to investigate the past.

I have written some background information for each unit, but all the evidence comes from people who were alive at the time or who have written about the event since that time. I have tried not to tell you what I think, but to let you make your own decisions about the past. Let's try this out!

Shortly after moving into an old house you discover a dusty box hidden away at the back of a cupboard under the stairs. It seems to be full of old newspapers and photographs. Your mum says that you and your friends can look through the box to try to find out who the owner might be.

In this unit you can see the first three items you took out of the box.

B

What sort of building is this?

C

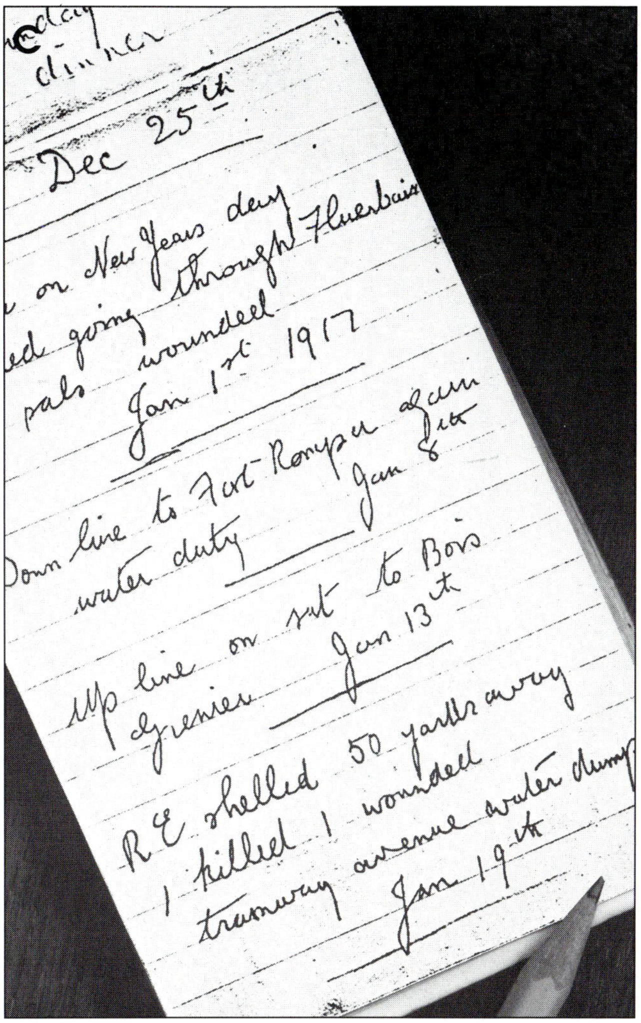

This is one section from a small blue book which you removed from the box. Written inside the front cover you find '64470 J.W. Maddison, 162nd Field Amb. R.A.M.C. France'.

What do you think this object might be?

CORE ACTIVITY

1 History is about what people have done in the past. Looking at each piece of evidence again, in turn:

- Make a list of what people were able to do at that time. (*CLUE TO SUCCESS*: Let's use evidence **B** as an example. Your list might begin: People could make buildings of stone.... Then you might write down what people would do in that particular building)

EXTENSION ACTIVITIES

1 History is about people, places and events.
- Which of the evidence in this unit tells us something about:
  - people
  - a place
  - an event?

2 Look carefully at each piece of evidence.
- Using any other books or material available to you, find out about:
  - the people
  - this sort of building
  - the event
- Which pieces of evidence were the most difficult to find out about?
- Why do you think this might be?

2. TIME AND CHRONOLOGY

Target

* To introduce you to ideas about time and chronology.

A

Time-line.

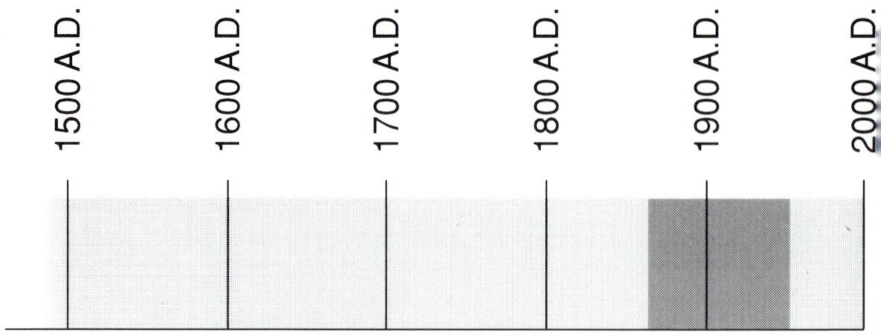

Time
In Unit 1 you learnt that history is about people and what they have done in the past. To understand the past we need to know something about TIME.

Throughout history the idea of time and how to record the passing of time has varied. In the Christian world we use the birth of Christ to mark the change from B.C. (before Christ) to A.D. (Anno Domini), which means in the year of our Lord. Muslims, who measure their time from an event in the life of Muhammad, would use A.H. (Anno Hegira).

Christians would say we are in 1990 A.D.
Muslims would say it is 1368 A.H.

B

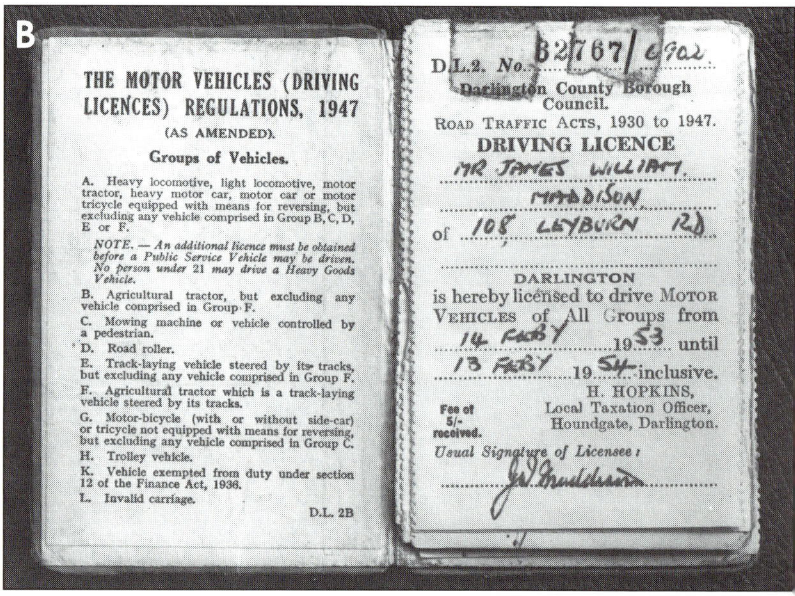
THE MOTOR VEHICLES (DRIVING LICENCES) REGULATIONS, 1947
(AS AMENDED).

Groups of Vehicles.

A. Heavy locomotive, light locomotive, motor tractor, heavy motor car, motor car or motor tricycle equipped with means for reversing, but excluding any vehicle comprised in Group B, C, D, E or F.

NOTE. — An additional licence must be obtained before a Public Service Vehicle may be driven. No person under 21 may drive a Heavy Goods Vehicle.

B. Agricultural tractor, but excluding any vehicle comprised in Group F.
C. Mowing machine or vehicle controlled by a pedestrian.
D. Road roller.
E. Track-laying vehicle steered by its tracks, but excluding any vehicle comprised in Group F.
F. Agricultural tractor which is a track-laying vehicle steered by its tracks.
G. Motor-bicycle (with or without side-car) or tricycle not equipped with means for reversing, but excluding any vehicle comprised in Group C.
H. Trolley vehicle.
K. Vehicle exempted from duty under section 12 of the Finance Act, 1936.
L. Invalid carriage.

D.L. 2B

D.L.2. No. B2767/6902
Darlington County Borough Council.
ROAD TRAFFIC ACTS, 1930 to 1947.
DRIVING LICENCE
MR JAMES WILLIAM
MADDISON
of 108 LEYBURN RD
DARLINGTON
is hereby licensed to drive MOTOR VEHICLES of All Groups from
14 FEBY 1953 until
13 FEBY 1954 inclusive.
H. HOPKINS,
Local Taxation Officer,
Houndgate, Darlington.
Fee of 5/- received.
Usual Signature of Licensee:

What is this item?

C

What event is being advertised?

You will find A.D. and B.C. used a lot in this book, so do make sure you know what they mean.

In the other books in this series you will find a time-line at the beginning of each unit. Marked on each time-line will be the position of the unit you are studying. Each time-line will look like the one shown in **A**. All the items on this page fit into the shaded time slot.

Chronology
CHRONOLOGY is a long word which simply means putting things in the order of time. In this unit you can see some more of the evidence from the box you found (Unit 1).

CORE ACTIVITIES

1 Look again at the part of this unit which is about chronology.
- Make a list of all the items in this unit, placing them in chronological order. (*CLUE TO SUCCESS*: Begin with the oldest item and end with the newest)

2 The unit of time you use to measure your own life is years.
- Using a scale of one centimetre for each year draw your own time-line similar to that in **A**.
- Mark on your time-line any important events in your life. (*CLUE TO SUCCESS*: You could mark on your time-line when you started school, when you learnt to swim, and so on)

What event do you think these people had visited?

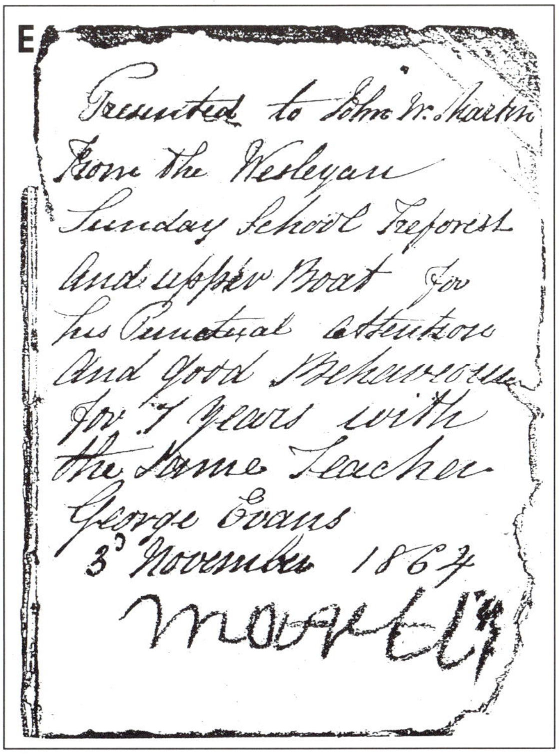

Presented to John W. Martin
From the Wesleyan
Sunday School Treforest
And upper Boat For
his Punctual attention
And good Behaviour
For 7 years with
the same Teacher
George Evans
3d November 1864

Who was this document presented to?

The words on the back of this photograph read 'Maurice and Olive aged 4 years'.

What might the relationship be between all the people on this photograph?

EXTENSION ACTIVITIES

1 Imagine you are stranded on a desert island without a clock or watch.
- Think of ways of measuring time.
- You might like to draw cartoons to show your ideas to other members of your group.

2 Why not try a chronology game.
- Find an old comic and choose a short story.
- Cut out the story and then cut it up into individual pictures. Mix these up and then try to sort them out into the correct chronological order.
- Let a friend try it out as well.

3. PERIODS AND CENTURIES

Target

* To understand how historians divide up time.

A

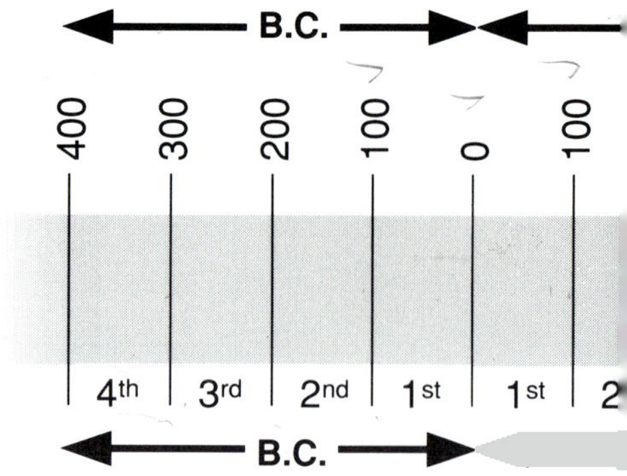

Time-line . 400 B.C. to Present.

Although all historians do not agree when human life first began to evolve (develop) on this earth, there is general agreement that modern humans evolved 42,000 years ago. To help us understand such a huge amount of time historians have split it up into periods.

The first 37,000 years is called the Prehistoric time. This means before recorded history, because during that time people had not developed the art of writing. Nearer to the present, we usually name periods of history after the people who were the rulers at that time. For example the Egyptians or the Tudors.

Historians also divide time into centuries. Each century is equal to one hundred years. We now live in the 1900s or the 20th century. **A** should help you understand how to work out which century certain years are in.

One of the problems with your box of evidence is that the items seem to come from different centuries and periods. The next three items you take from the box are **B, C** and **D**. You can see these in this unit.

B

Beaumaris Castle built in 1300s. Summer 1985.

? *What do you think the date Summer 1985 might mean?*

CORE ACTIVITY

1 You will need to make a copy of **A** but only write the centuries from the bottom of the diagram on to your time-line.
- Put the items in this unit into the correct century on your time-line.
- Look through the other units in this book and add other pieces of evidence to your time-line. Again make sure you put them in the correct century.

Checking Your Progress!
Ask a friend to check that you have placed all the evidence in the correct century. You could also check your friend's progress.

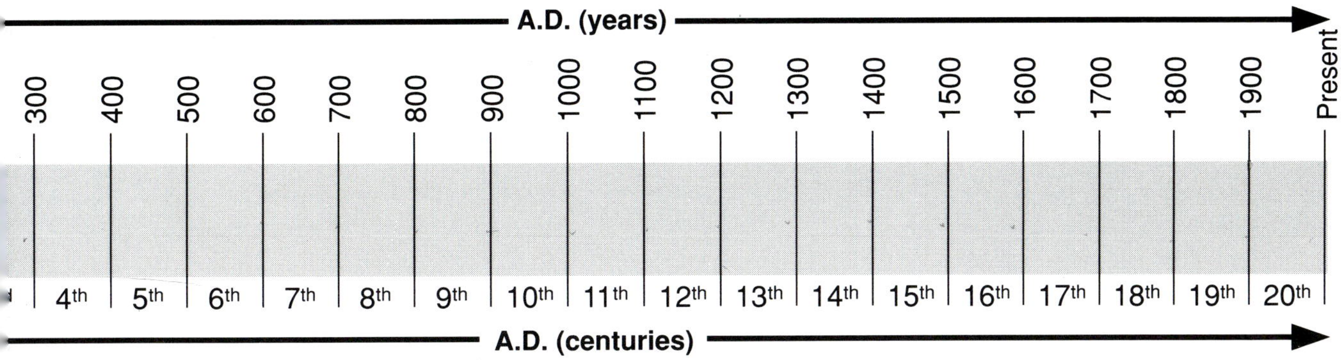

C

Nov. 28th Owing to the unsettled and cold state of the ~~att~~ weather the attendance for the week is four short of the average of last week.
Yesterday I had occasion to punish a boy rather severely for disobedience. Subsequently the boy's mother visited the school and threatened to send him to some other school.
Taught the first verse of the melody "Star of Peace" and the tune.

Try to read this extract with your friends.

? *Can you find the exact date when this extract was written?*

? *What event is shown on this photograph?*

EXTENSION ACTIVITIES

1 • Brainstorm as many different names of periods in history as possible. When you get stuck compare your answers with a friend.

2 • Using any books which are available to you try to discover other historical periods and find out which century each period was in.
• You could write these periods on your time-line too.

3 • Try to find out which period each of the items on this page is from.

4. HOW DO WE KNOW?

Target

* To understand how historians find out about the past.
* To introduce you to primary and secondary evidence.

In this section we need to think about how historians actually find out about the past. If you want to know about something which happened in your family before you were born, you would probably ask your mum or dad. In order to answer your questions they might need to look at some family photographs, talk to older relatives or hunt out some family documents. So we find out about history by looking at the evidence left behind by people of the past. This is called PRIMARY evidence.

A

Photographic evidence: Jimmy 1917.

What do you think these men did?

B

TRY SOME TODAY! SOVEREIGN Creamy Whirls

DAILY HERALD

No. 12656 (C) WEATHER: Dry, sunny periods.—See Page 5. RADIO and TV—See Page 5 PRICE 2d

GREEN GODDESS Her Favourite Drink

Cease-fire at midnight: But Egypt says 'We fight on'

EDEN CALLS IT OFF

BRITAIN and France have stopped fighting in Egypt. A cease-fire started at midnight. British troops will stay where they are.

Britain and France accept the idea of an international force to police the Middle East. They abandon their demands that their troops should form part of that force and that the United Nations should impose the Anglo-French solution on Colonel Nasser.

Egypt last night called for a special meeting of the General Assembly of the United Nations. It was taking place at 2.30 this morning.

The Egyptians called on Britain, France and Israel to withdraw all their forces. And Cairo Radio said there could be no end to the fighting until all the "aggressors" had left.

A storm of Labour cheers greeted Sir Anthony Eden when he announced the news of the cease-fire in the House of Commons.

He said that if Egypt and Israel stopped fighting so would Britain and France. Allied troops would not advance southward. And technicians with the armies would at once begin clearing the blocked Canal.

The British Cabinet had been in session for three and three-quarter hours, obviously disagreeing. They suffered a withering attack by Hugh Gaitskell.

At 6 o'clock Sir Anthony rose to announce his major climb-down. His policy was in ruins. But his Cabinet, for the time, was intact.

What happens now to the British troops in Egypt? Nobody knows yet—except that they are unlikely to stay long. A United Nations force, in which there will be no British, French, Russian or U.S. troops, will take over.

Labour MPs cheer dramatic switch in Tory policy

By HUGH PILCHER, Parliamentary Correspondent

IT was a tense, packed Commons which Sir Anthony Eden faced as he stood up to announce last night that, subject to acceptance by Egypt and Israel of an unconditional cease-fire, the "armed conflict" in Suez

WHAT WE SAY

PUBLIC opinion led courageously and decisively by the Labour Party, wins a mighty victory.

The people have forced Eden to capitulate to United Nations, to the great moral authority which he spurned and upon which, in recent days, his supporters in Parliament and the Press have poured contempt and scorn.

Even the conditions to which Eden's Foreign Secretary clung

VICTORY

that cannot be the end; the British people dare not ignore the cost of Eden's folly.

Our moral authority in the world has been destroyed.

The strength of the Anglo - American alliance has been impaired.

The unity of the British Commonwealth has been endangered.

The blood — spilled needlessly — of many human be-

Planes blast Budapest but still rebels fight

From ALFRED RICHMAN On the Austro-Hungarian Border, Tuesday

WAVE after wave of Red Air Force planes bombed Budapest West station today, and 200,000 Soviet troops with 4,600 tanks were reported to have moved into Hungary. **But the rebels are fighting on.**

Russians are hanging prisoners from the Danube bridges in the capital. Artillery is shelling rebel strongholds from the heights of Buda.

But still they fight on.

That was the word tonight, from refugees still trickling over the border, and from the will-o'-the-wisp freedom radio stations which are defying all Russian attempts to [illegible] them.

In a minute

One rebel radio transmitter using the call-sign "Fox" reported that after a fierce fight the Hungarians had recaptured Parliament building.

Late this afternoon another station, "Radio Rokoczky," made a desperate appeal for guns, ammunition and food to be parachuted to Dunapentele—an industrial city 40 miles south of Budapest.

on us to lay down our arms," it said. "We will not comply. Arms, ammunition, medicine and food—please drop them.

Thirty minutes later, "Radio Rokoczky" announced: "Four Russian tanks have just attacked Dunapentele. The garrison opened artillery fire on them, and in the first minute all four surrendered."

A refugee from Budapest said that rebel Hungarian soldiers who surrendered were being given the "concession" of being shot instead of hanged.

Mongolians?

Afterwards they were hung up on lamp-posts with placards pinned to them saying: "This is the fate of all capitalists."

Another report reaching Austria says that the Russians are using Mongolian troops in the capital.

US says Hands off Austria

AMERICA warned Russia yesterday that any attempt to violate the territorial integrity and internal sovereignty of Austria would be considered "a grave threat to world [illegible]"

The U.S. denounced as "grossly false" a Russian charge in UNO that "persons sponsored by America and operating from Austria" had supported the Hungarian revolt.

FRANCE'S Premier, M. Guy Mollet, replied to Marshal Bulganin's threat of force in the Middle East.

"I doubt," he said, "that the Soviet has the right to express its pity for 'innocent blood' when such blood is

Written evidence. A newspaper is just one form of written evidence.

Historians investigate the past using primary evidence. Then they write their own interpretation (account) of what might have happened. An account written by a historian is called SECONDARY evidence.

Most of the evidence in this book is primary evidence. You will be asked to look at the primary evidence carefully and then put together your own ideas about what might have happened. Your ideas or interpretation will be secondary evidence.

The evidence in this unit is also from the box which was discovered under the stairs. You will see that there are many different types of primary evidence which you can use to find out about the past.

CORE ACTIVITIES

1 Look carefully at **A.**
- What can you learn about people in 1917 from this photograph?

2 Newspapers are an important source of written evidence.
- Make a list of what you can learn about the past from newspapers.

3 **C** shows you one artefact.
- Can you think of other examples of artefacts?

C

Artefacts: arm badge 1917.
An artefact is an object made by human beings.

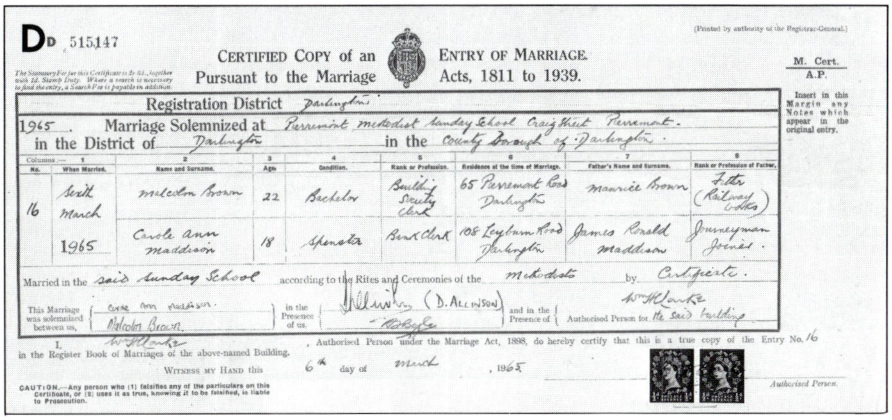
D 515147

CERTIFIED COPY of an ENTRY OF MARRIAGE.
Pursuant to the Marriage Acts, 1811 to 1939.

M. Cert. A.P.

Registration District Darlington

1965. Marriage Solemnized at Pierremont Methodist Sunday School Craig Street Pierremont. in the District of Darlington in the County Borough of Darlington.

No.	When Married.	Name and Surname.	Age.	Condition.	Rank or Profession.	Residence at the time of Marriage.	Father's Name and Surname.	Rank or Profession of Father.
16	Sixth March 1965	Malcolm Brown	22	Bachelor	Building Society Clerk	65 Pierremont Road Darlington	Maurice Brown	Fitter (Railway Works)
		Carole Ann Maddison	18	Spinster	Bank Clerk	108 Leyburn Road Darlington	James Ronald Maddison	Journeyman Joiner

Married in the said Sunday School according to the Rites and Ceremonies of the Methodists by Certificate.

This Marriage was solemnized between us, Carole Ann Maddison. Malcolm Brown. in the Presence of us, (D. ALLINSON) and in the Presence of Authorised Person for the said building

Authorised Person under the Marriage Act, 1898, do hereby certify that this is a true copy of the Entry No. 16 in the Register Book of Marriages of the above-named Building.

WITNESS MY HAND this 6th day of March, 1965

Official documents. These records must be completed by law.

? What is this document?

E

Buildings.

? How do you think this building might be used?

4 Look at **D**.

- What can you learn from it?

5 Buildings can provide a lot of evidence about how people used to live.

- Can you think of other types of buildings?

6 **F** shows memorabilia.

- What can you learn from **F**?
- What sort of memorabilia do you keep?
- You might like to discuss your answers to these questions with your friends.

F

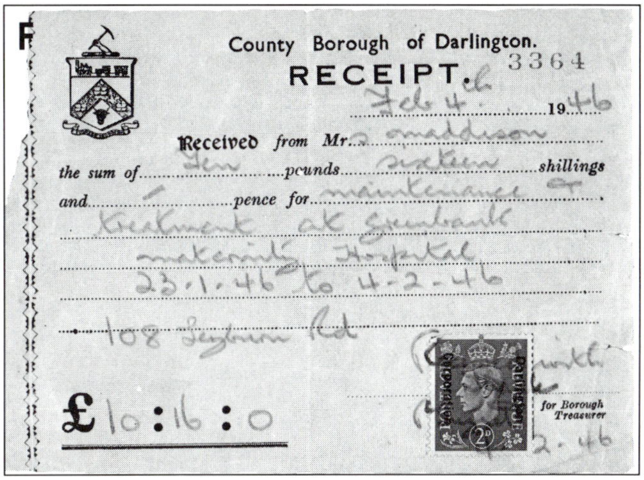
County Borough of Darlington.
RECEIPT. 3364

Feb 4 1946

Received from Mr. Maddison

the sum of Ten pounds sixteen shillings and — pence for maintenance & treatment at Greenbank maternity Hospital 23.1.46 to 4-2-46

108 Leyburn Rd

£10 : 16 : 0

for Borough Treasurer

Memorabilia: items which are usually thrown away. Sometimes kept to remind people of a certain event.

EXTENSION ACTIVITIES

1 Look carefully at the primary evidence in this unit.

- Can you spot any links or connections which one piece of evidence has with another?

2 Try to find some primary evidence at home or in your classroom.

- Write your own interpretation of the evidence.
- Is your interpretation primary or secondary evidence?
  (*CLUE TO SUCCESS*: Think about what you can learn about people of the past from your primary evidence?)

3 ● Working with a friend draw up a list of primary evidence you would try to find in order to learn about the following:
- castles - First World War

5. ASKING HISTORICAL QUESTIONS

Target.

* To learn how to ask historical questions.

You will remember that in Unit 1 I said that finding out about history is like a journey of adventure into the past. Now I want to suggest that it is a detective adventure. This means that you will have to learn to examine historical evidence very carefully and then ask the right questions in order to find out more. Already you are used to asking questions of your parents, teachers and friends, but the problem with historical questions is that often the people you wish to speak to are no longer alive. You have to be able to look at different types of evidence and think of the questions you would ask the people if you could speak to them.

Once you have learnt the questions you need to ask you can apply them to any evidence from the past to help you piece together a picture of what might have happened.

Remember though we can rarely be really sure about what happened. At best you will only be able to put together your own ideas or your own interpretation of the evidence and events. Let's try this out!

A and **B** are some more items from your box. I have added labels which suggest questions you might ask, but I am sure that you will be able to think of many more.

A

CORE ACTIVITIES

1 Supposing you were able to meet the lady in photograph **A.**

- Working with your friends make a list of all the questions you would like to ask her.
  (*CLUE TO SUCCESS*: You might like to try a brainstorm but remember, no one should be left out and no one should be ignored)

2 **B** provides evidence of a national event.

- Try to write out your own list of historical questions which you might ask about this evidence. I have drawn in some arrows to help you with your questions.

B

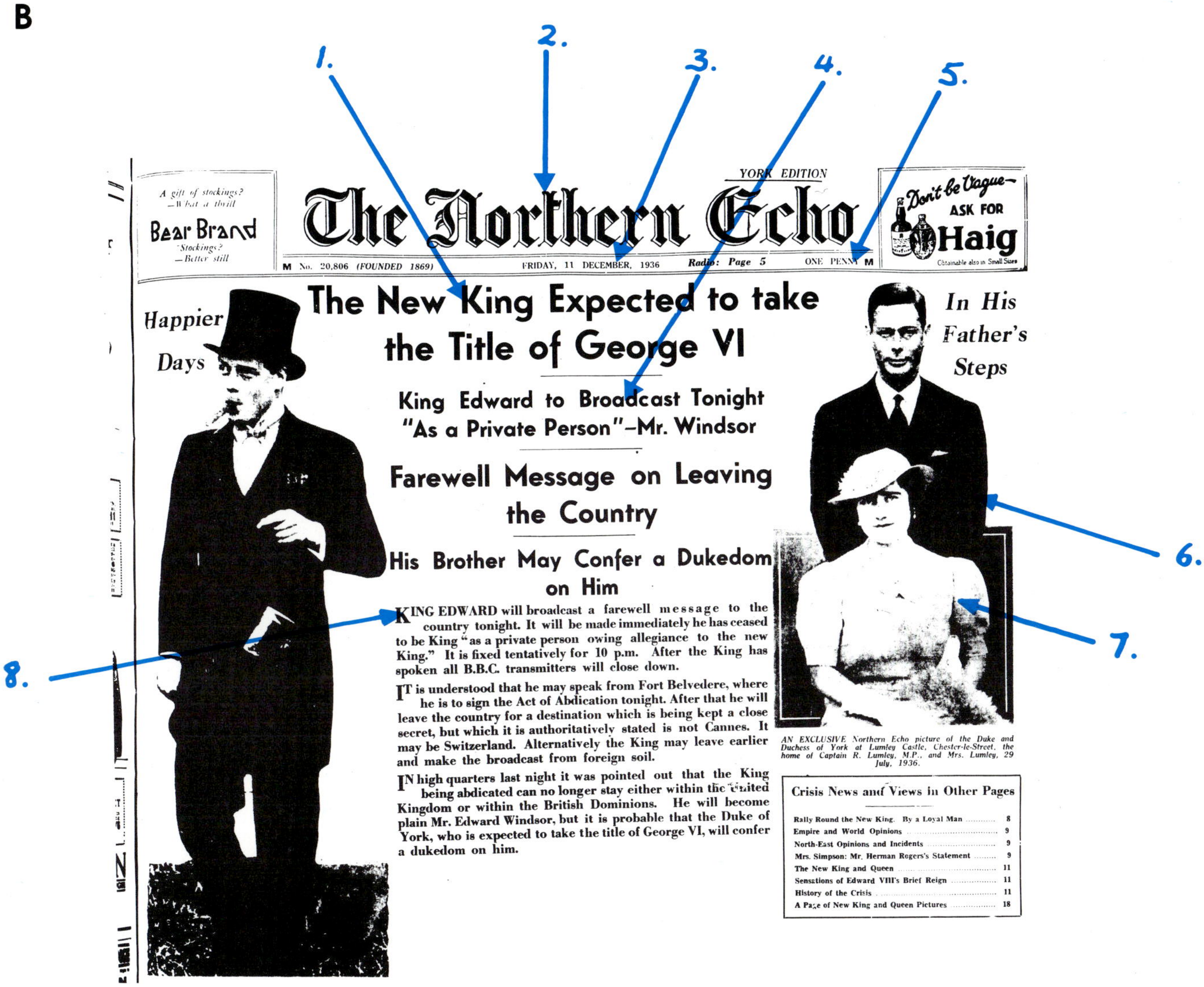

A gift of stockings? —What a thrill
Bear Brand Stockings? —Better still

YORK EDITION

The Northern Echo

Don't be Vague— ASK FOR Haig
Obtainable also in Small Sizes

M No. 20,806 (FOUNDED 1869) FRIDAY, 11 DECEMBER, 1936 Radio: Page 5 ONE PENNY M

The New King Expected to take the Title of George VI

King Edward to Broadcast Tonight "As a Private Person"—Mr. Windsor

Farewell Message on Leaving the Country

His Brother May Confer a Dukedom on Him

KING EDWARD will broadcast a farewell message to the country tonight. It will be made immediately he has ceased to be King "as a private person owing allegiance to the new King." It is fixed tentatively for 10 p.m. After the King has spoken all B.B.C. transmitters will close down.

IT is understood that he may speak from Fort Belvedere, where he is to sign the Act of Abdication tonight. After that he will leave the country for a destination which is being kept a close secret, but which it is authoritatively stated is not Cannes. It may be Switzerland. Alternatively the King may leave earlier and make the broadcast from foreign soil.

IN high quarters last night it was pointed out that the King being abdicated can no longer stay either within the United Kingdom or within the British Dominions. He will become plain Mr. Edward Windsor, but it is probable that the Duke of York, who is expected to take the title of George VI, will confer a dukedom on him.

Happier Days

In His Father's Steps

AN EXCLUSIVE Northern Echo picture of the Duke and Duchess of York at Lumley Castle, Chester-le-Street, the home of Captain R. Lumley, M.P., and Mrs. Lumley, 29 July, 1936.

Crisis News and Views in Other Pages

Rally Round the New King. By a Loyal Man 8
Empire and World Opinions 9
North-East Opinions and Incidents 9
Mrs. Simpson: Mr. Herman Rogers's Statement 9
The New King and Queen 11
Sensations of Edward VIII's Brief Reign 11
History of the Crisis 11
A Page of New King and Queen Pictures 18

3 Imagine you can interview any of the people named in the newspaper.
- Who would you choose to interview?
- What would you ask them?

Checking Your Progress!
Probably many of the questions you have asked began with the letter 'W'. For example, what? who? when? where? why?
I hope that you have also used the word 'how'. Of course these are not the only words you can use to begin questions, but they are helpful words to remember when working with historical evidence.

EXTENSION ACTIVITIES

1 Look again at **A** and **B.**
- Can you think of any other questions to ask?

2 Try to find out more about the people and events shown by both the sources.
- Which source was it easiest to find out more about?
- Why do you think it was it easier to find out more about one source than the other?

6. FINDING OUT FROM PICTURES

Target

* To learn to observe, describe and interpret visual evidence.

You have already looked at some photographs from your box. In this unit you can see two more photographs.

What sort of shop is shown in this photograph?

Some of the first evidence left behind by people of the past were drawings. These were made thousands of years before people were able to write. In fact, the first writing was made up of small drawings called hieroglyphics. The drawings left behind by early people provide important evidence about how they lived, what they looked like and what ideas they believed in.

Later in history people left behind paintings. They engraved pictures into stone and made figures of people from marble. Since the middle of the 1800s, when the camera was invented, photographs have also provided a lot of evidence about the past. During the 20th century, movie film, television and video film have been used to record past events. All these pictures of the past can help us to learn about people at the time.

CORE ACTIVITIES

(*CLUE TO SUCCESS*: When using pictures as historical evidence you need to observe all the details very carefully. If you were reading a book, you would read from the top of the page downwards. Try to think about reading pictures in the same way)

1 Working with a partner look carefully at **A**.

- Beginning in the top left hand corner of the photograph describe carefully to your partner what you can see. Here are some questions to start you off:
  - What building materials have been used?
  - What do you notice about the way the people are dressed?
  - What is the name of the shop?

  Now continue to describe to your partner what you can see in the picture.
  Be sure that you work down the picture and include as many details as possible.

B

The words 'Robert Barker wounded 1915' are written on the back of this photograph.

2 You now have to interpret the evidence. In other words you must explain what you can learn about people who lived at the time photo A was taken. (*CLUE TO SUCCESS*: One way of interpreting evidence is to ask questions)

- Here are some questions to help you.
  - Could people read and write?
  - Did they have a money system?
  - Did they have a Royal Family at the time?
  - Were they able to construct buildings?
- You will need a copy of **C**. Put your answers to these questions in the Answer Box.
- Make sure that you explain how you know by filling in the Supporting Evidence Box.
- Make a list of anything else you can learn about people at the time from this photograph.

3 Choose one of the people shown in **A**.

- Write a brief account of the work he or she might be expected to do in the shop.

C

Question	Answer Box	Supporting Evidence Box
a) Could people read and write?		
b) Did they have a money system?		
c) Was there outdoor lighting?		
d) Were they able to construct buildings?		

EXTENSION ACTIVITIES

1 **B** is another photograph from your box. You can try out your skills of observation, description and interpretation again.

- Look carefully at **B**.
- Describe in detail the photograph, beginning at the top.
- Write a list of what you can learn about people at the time from the photograph. (*CLUE TO SUCCESS*: Think about these questions: What job does this man do? What skills must people have had in order to make his uniform? Why do you think photographs like this were taken and sent home?)

2 In order to become really good at finding out from pictures you need lots of practice.

- See if you can find an old photograph of your own family.
- Try to find one showing some of your relatives standing outside the house in which they lived.
- Now have a go at the following:
  - Look carefully at the photograph, then write out a detailed description.
  - Ask yourself what you can learn about people at the time from your photograph.
- Write a list of your answers.

3 Look carefully at the people shown on your photograph.

- Can you suggest how your life might be different to theirs?
- What clues in the photograph help you to decide when it might have been taken?

7. USING WRITTEN EVIDENCE

Target

* To learn how to use written evidence.

The most common type of evidence which historians use is written or documentary evidence. A document is any sort of written evidence from the past which has been kept or preserved.

You have already looked at some written evidence from your box in other units.
You might have noticed that there are many different types of written evidence. For example, **C** in Unit 1 is a page from a diary written by a soldier during the First World War. This is a private or family document. Family letters, bills and accounts are also examples of private documents.

The driving licence in Unit 2 is an example of a legal document, as the law states that every driver of a motor vehicle must hold a driving licence.
C in Unit 2 is a church document, while the school log book in Unit 3 is an example of a Parish document. Local newspapers, like the one you can see in Unit 5, also provide written evidence.

To build up a picture of what might have happened in the past you need to learn how to use written evidence. In this unit you can see two pieces of written evidence which you have taken from your box. Before moving on to the activities, read **A** and **B** carefully.

A

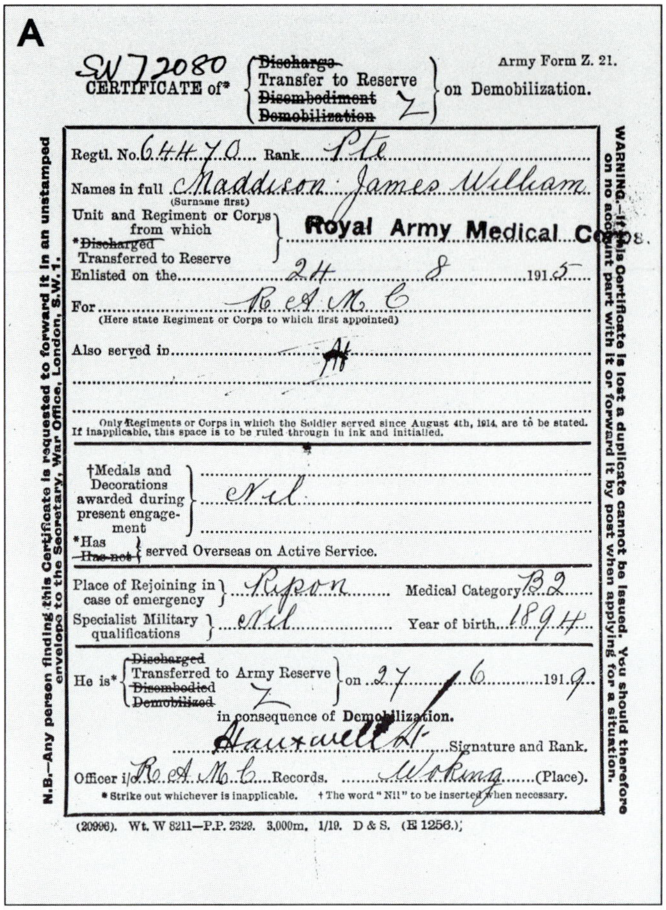

SW 72080

CERTIFICATE of* ~~Discharge~~ / Transfer to Reserve / ~~Disembodiment~~ / ~~Demobilization~~ on Demobilization. Army Form Z. 21.

Regtl. No. 64470 Rank Pte

Names in full Maddison James William (Surname first)

Unit and Regiment or Corps from which *~~Discharged~~ Transferred to Reserve: Royal Army Medical Corps.

Enlisted on the 24 8 1915

For R A M C (Here state Regiment or Corps to which first appointed)

Also served in

Only Regiments or Corps in which the Soldier served since August 4th, 1914, are to be stated. If inapplicable, this space is to be ruled through in ink and initialled.

†Medals and Decorations awarded during present engagement: Nil

*Has ~~Has not~~ served Overseas on Active Service.

Place of Rejoining in case of emergency: Ripon   Medical Category B2

Specialist Military qualifications: Nil   Year of birth 1894

He is* ~~Discharged~~ Transferred to Army Reserve ~~Disembodied~~ ~~Demobilized~~ on 27 6 1919 in consequence of Demobilization.

Signature and Rank.

Officer i/c R A M C Records. Woking (Place).

* Strike out whichever is inapplicable. † The word "Nil" to be inserted when necessary.

(20996). Wt. W 8211—P.P. 2329. 3,000m. 1/19. D & S. (E 1256.)

N.B.—Any person finding this Certificate is requested to forward it in an unstamped envelope to the Secretary, War Office, London, S.W.1.

WARNING.—If this Certificate is lost a duplicate cannot be issued. You should therefore on no account part with it or forward it by post when applying for a situation.

What is this document?

CORE ACTIVITIES

1 Translating a document or writing it out in your own words can often give you a better understanding of what it is about. The following questions will help you to build up your own translation of **A**.
- What is the number of the certificate?
- Write out the following:
  - Regulation number
  - Rank
  - Names in full
  - Unit and regiment or corps
  - Date enlisted

2 Look again at **A**.
- Which regiment or corps was this soldier first appointed to?
- Did he win any medals or decorations? How do you know?
- In what year was the soldier born?
- What date was he transferred to the Army Reserve?

B

Contracts of Employment Act 1963

Date 10/9/64

THIS STATEMENT SETS OUT PARTICULARS OF THE TERMS AND CONDITIONS ON WHICH:-

(Name of Employer) William Brown's Saw Mills Ltd. employs (Name of Employee) MADDISON. James, Ronald. (306)

Your employment began on 11:5:64 and you are paid at weekly intervals.

Scale or rate of remuneration, or the method of calculating remuneration 6/1½ per hour plus bonus of 6d per hour paid one week in arrears. Overtime calculated in accordance with the National Agreement of the Joint Council for the Building Industries.

Normal hours of work, and any other terms and conditions relating to hours of work Normal hours 42 hours per week.
~~Mon. to Wed.~~ 7.45 a.m. to 12.10 p.m. with tea break from 9.50 a.m. to 10.00 a.m.
1 p.m. to 5.15 p.m. with tea break 3.00 p.m. to 3.10 p.m.
Thurs. & Fri. as above but finish at 5.00 p.m. not 5.15 p.m.

Holidays and holiday pay Annual and Public Holidays as per the agreements for the Building and Civil Engineering Contracting Industries.

Terms and conditions relating to incapacity for work due to sickness or injury, and sick pay A Sick Note is to be handed to the Wages Department at the earliest opportunity in order to qualify for a Holiday Stamp.

Pensions and pension schemes No provision

Amount of notice of termination by (a) employer and (b) employee (a) ONE WEEK
(b) One week.

Other information Any changes in the above conditions will be entered on the Personal Record Card held in the Wages Department within one month of the change, and is open to inspection at any reasonable time.

This is a Contract of Employment.

? *Who was the owner of the saw mill?*

? *What was the name of the employee?*

3 Look at the printing down the left side of the certificate.
- In your own words write out the sentence which follows the letters: 'N.B.'.
- What warning is printed down the right side of the certificate?

4 To understand the document even more you need to ask certain questions. Here are some to help you.
- Why was this certificate written? (*CLUE TO SUCCESS*: Find out what the word 'demobilization' means)
- Why do you think the soldier was being transferred to the Army Reserve?

5 This certificate is more than 70 years old.
- Why do you think it has been carefully preserved by the soldier's family?

Checking Your Progress!
Compare your answers to questions 1 to 5 with those of a friend. If any of your answers disagree, look again at the sources and try to agree whose answer is right.

EXTENSION ACTIVITIES

1 ● In your own words write a report on the working conditions of James Ronald Maddison at Brown's Saw Mills in 1964. You should include information on:
- rates of pay
- hours of work
- holidays
- sickness or injury
- any other information

You could work with a partner for this activity.

2 As a historian you would need more evidence to help you build up a picture of working life in the 1960s. This is called supporting evidence.
- Try showing the Contract of Employment to one of your grandparents or someone who was working at that time. Ask them to tell you about their working life and compare the information with the report you wrote about **A**.

8. LEARNING FROM ARTEFACTS

Targets

* To develop the skills needed to learn from artefacts.

An artefact is an object which has been made by human beings. It is another sort of historical evidence from which we can learn a great deal about the past.

This artefact is made out of silver.
Written on the front is 'GEORGIVS V D.G.BRITT: OMN:REX F.D. IND:IMP:'.

? *What is this artefact?*

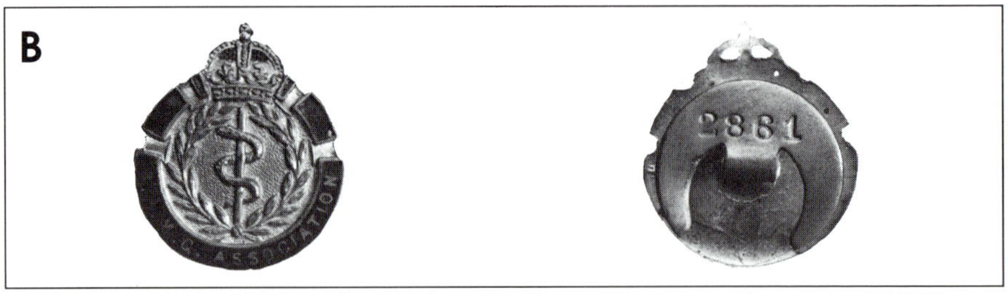

Here you can see both sides of this artefact. These numbers read 2861.
On the front of the artefact the writing reads 'R.A.M.C. Association'.

? *What might the words mean?*

These artefacts are probably made of bronze. Printed on the back of this one is '411710 James W. Maddison'. There was one of these for each year up to 1962.

? *What was the interest of the owner of these medals?*

As you work through this book you will find many artefacts from different periods of history. From each artefact you can learn something about the people who made it and what life might have been like at the time. Many of the skills which you learnt in other units can be used when studying artefacts. You will need to observe and describe carefully, as you did when finding out from pictures. You will also have to ask questions about the artefacts.

You have seen several artefacts in earlier units. For example in Unit 4 you looked at the Arm Badge. In this unit you can look at photographs of some other artefacts which you found in your box. The photographs show what the artefacts look like but because you can't actually handle them, a little further information has been provided for you. Sometimes details of the materials used to make the artefact have been given. At other times, any words printed on the artefacts which might have been too small for you to read, have been written out.

Have a good look at the artefacts. Imagine you can actually handle them, turning them over to look at the backs and the fronts. Try to imagine how heavy each one might feel in your hand.

This artefact is made from a very heavy metal, probably cast iron.

What questions might you ask about this artefact?

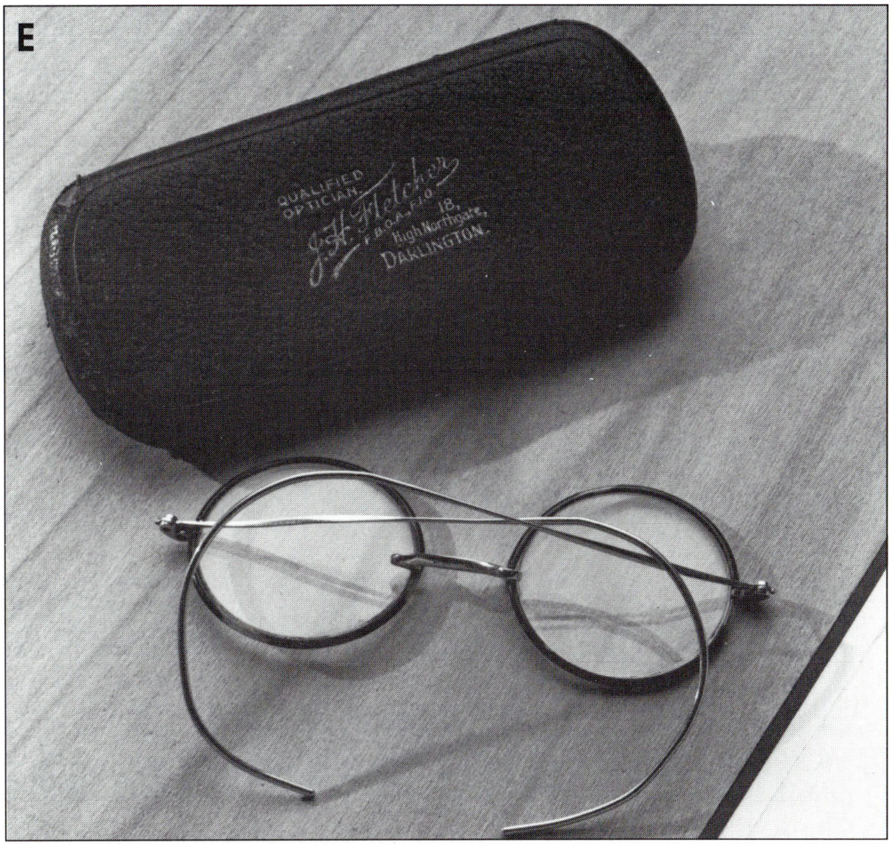

The legs of these glasses and the nose section are made from a very fine, light metal. The lenses are made from glass. This is the case. It is lined with purple velvet. This photograph shows the bottom of the case.

In which century might these glasses have been made?

CORE ACTIVITIES

1 Look carefully at **A** then complete the following:
- Draw the artefact.
- Write a detailed description about everything you can see on each side of the artefact. Don't forget to mention shape and colour.
- Explain what you can learn about the people who made the artefact and life at the time.
  EXAMPLE: You might say the people had money, they could read and write, there was a king.

2 Now, looking at **C** and **D** in turn:
- Do all parts of Activity 1 again.

EXTENSION ACTIVITIES

1 Investigate the artefacts shown in **B** and **E** by answering the following questions for each artefact.
- What is it?
- What was its purpose?
- How was it used?
- When might it have been made and how do you know?
- What sort of person might have made the artefact?
- How was it made?
- What difference might the artefact have made to the lives of those who used it?
- What can you learn about people of that time from the artefact?

2 Try to find an artefact at home which is quite old.
- Make a sketch of the artefact and then answer the questions set in Activity 1.
- What other questions might you ask about the artefact?
- Why not take your work into school, together with the artefact, to show your teacher or friends.

9. TALKING WITH PEOPLE

Target

* To learn how to collect oral evidence.

Some of the most important sources of evidence from the recent past are people's memories of their lives. There are many people alive today who are 80 or 90 years old. A few people are over 100 years old! Imagine all the things which must have happened to someone aged about 80 years. They would be born very near the beginning of this century, perhaps in 1907 or 1908, before either of the World Wars, when very few people had cars and aircraft were just being developed. Even people like your grandparents, who might only be about 50 years old, would have many memories about their early life.

A

The school which was the Infants School, was set out with square tables with 4 chairs round each table.
There were no school dinners.

The outside of the school was made out of red bricks with tall windows, but you could not see out of the windows from the inside.
The boys and girls playgrounds were separated.

The lessons that were taught were arithmetic, reading, writing, sewing, geography, history and P.E. The children were scared stiff of most of the teachers. You had to remember some and write some things down. If you did not understand you got rattled (round the head or on the knuckles)

School was opened at 9.00 in the morning till 12.00, then at 1.00 to 4.00.

Read this carefully. Check with a friend or your teacher if there are any words you cannot read or do not understand.

By talking with people who have been alive for many years we can find out a great deal about local life. We can also find out about international events and how these might have affected people in our own area. It is also possible to compare differences between life as it is now and as it was in the past.

The main problem is how to collect people's memories so that a record of the past can be left for future generations. In this unit we are going to look at ways in which you can begin your own collection of oral (spoken) evidence.

Of course there was no oral evidence in your box, but you did find some evidence which was written as if the person was actually speaking. You can see it in this unit. Read it carefully.

CORE ACTIVITIES

1 As you might have guessed **A** seems to be answers to questions.
- Write out the questions which you think the person might have been asked.

2 Let's try an interview. (*CLUE TO SUCCESS*: You should try to make up questions which will encourage the person you are interviewing to talk)
EXAMPLE: A good question would be: 'What subjects did you study at school?' This is a good question because it cannot be answered with a 'yes' or a 'no'. A bad question would be: 'Did you study maths?'.
- Choose a topic you would like to interview a friend about. For example, their junior school; last holiday; hobbies etc.
- Write out a list of about 5 questions. Make sure that these questions cannot just be answered with a yes or no.
- Find a friend and ask if you can interview them about your chosen topic.
- Write down their answers to your questions.
- Finally write a short paragraph explaining what was difficult about writing down their answers.

EXTENSION ACTIVITIES

1 Collecting oral evidence involves several stages:

- Discuss with your teacher the topic you are going to research. (*CLUE TO SUCCESS*: **A** and **B** might give you some ideas)
- Write out your questions.
- Find a suitable person to interview. For example one of your grandparents or great grandparents. Your parents, too, will be able to help. You might have an elderly friend of the family who will let you interview them.
- Think about how you are going to keep an accurate record of their answers.
  You could use any of the following:
  - Listen carefully and remember the answers. (You need a very good memory for this.)
  - Write all the answers down. (Can you write quickly enough?)
  - Record the answers on a cassette tape.

  (You must remember to ask permission first as a lot of older people do not like having their voice recorded. Also you either need a battery operated cassette recorder or a power point you can use.)
- Which method of collecting evidence do you think would be the most reliable?

2 When you have conducted the interview bring the evidence you have collected back into school.

- Discuss with your teacher how you might display your findings.

B

left. There was very little change in the lives of women during the war years the 14-18 war I mean as far as I know everyone in our village were occupied with their families and homes just carrying on hoping for the war to end as a lot of women lost their son's and husbands, then of course there were air raids, I remember mum and dad going out as usual at weekends the boys all started going out too, as they needed their recreation and sport, I was left with the younger ones, now she would say "there might be an air raid" if there is, the buzzer at the pit will blow five minutes, the gas light will be lowered, so gather the bairns up, and get underneath the big table, piling all the cushions on top in case of flying glass, when the gas light goes back up again, and the buzzer at the pit blows again you know the raid is over. We could hear the planes going over and one night a Zeppelin, but of course they concentrated on the coastal areas, after that we

? *What international event is this source about?*

10. LOOKING AT MAPS

Target

* To learn how to use maps as historical evidence.

Maps are an important source of historical evidence. You can find out how places have changed over the years by comparing an old map with how that area looks today. It is also possible to learn when certain features were first built. For example a parish church or an old castle.

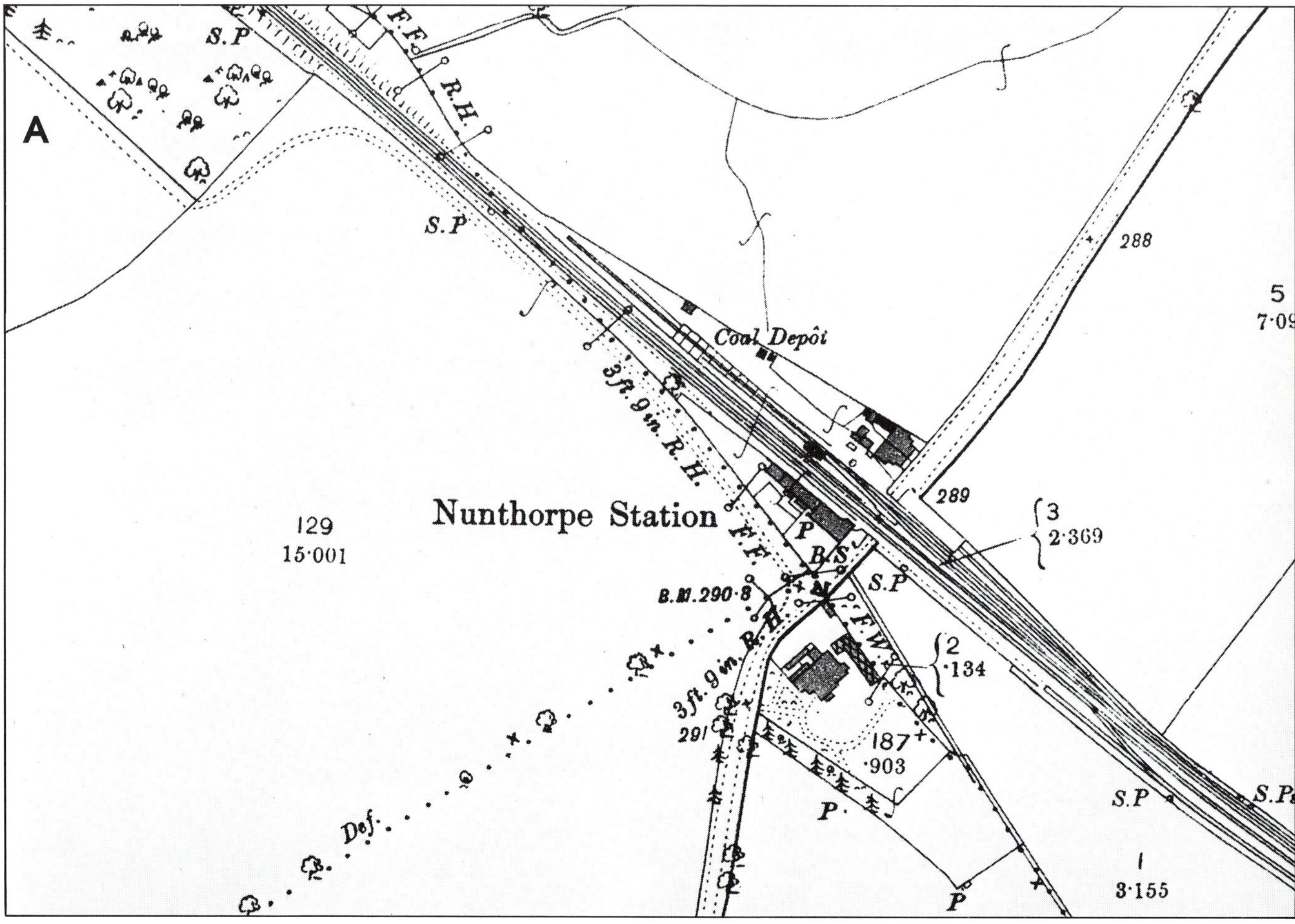

Ordnance Survey map 1894.

There are several different types of map which you will be looking at in these books. Some of the earliest maps were produced in the 1400s at the request of the government or for use in court cases. They were often drawn to show the ownership of land.

During the 1500s printed maps of some towns and cities were made and in the 1600s John Speed drew maps of over 70 towns.

You have probably heard of Ordnance Survey maps. These first appeared in 1801 and, because they have continued ever since, it is possible to build up a picture of changes in a village or town by looking at maps from different dates.

Tithe maps can be found for many areas after 1836. A tithe was an amount paid to the church and a map was necessary to work out how much each person should pay. These maps can provide a great deal of information about land, houses, streams, shops, paths and roads in a village or town.

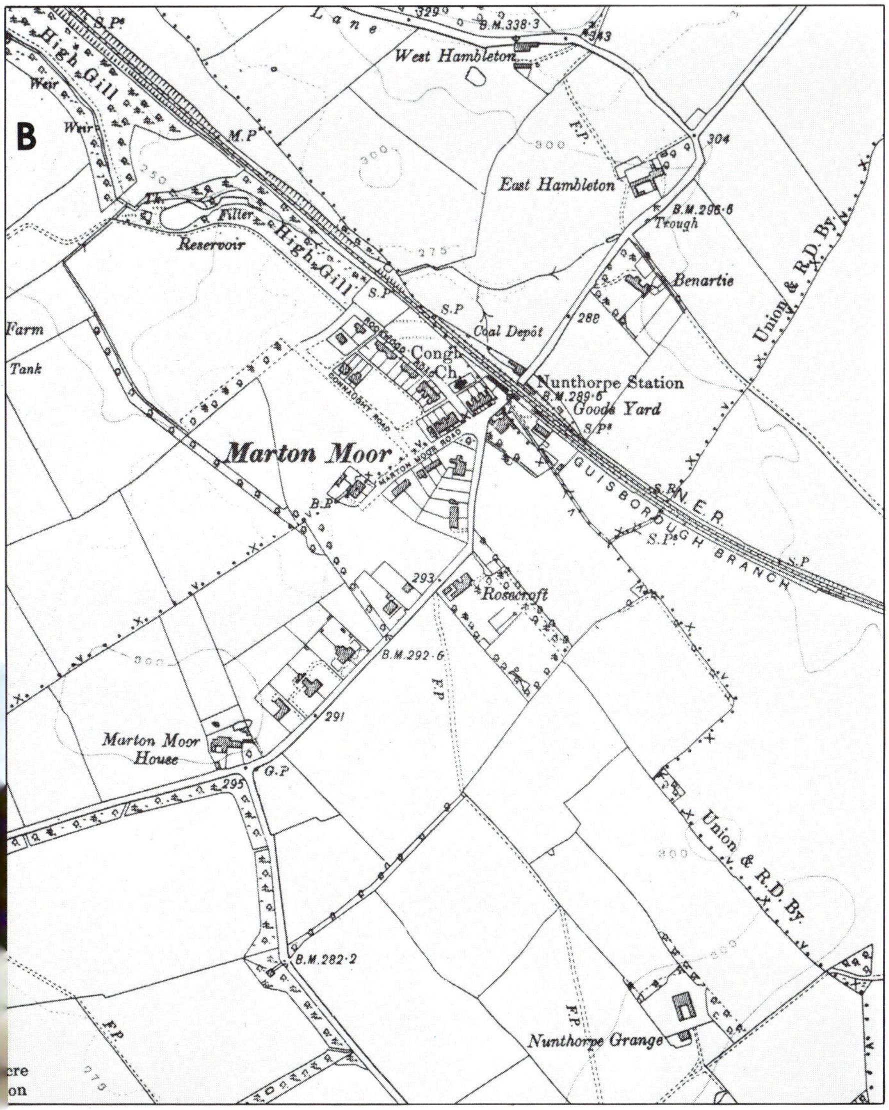

Ordnance Survey map 1919.

CORE ACTIVITIES

1 Look carefully at **A**.
- In what year was this edition of the map printed?
- What building is shown on this map?

2 Look at the railway line which runs from the left side of the map to the right side.
- Using other clues on the map explain what goods you think might have been carried by the railway. Give reasons for your answer.
- Using the map write a description of the area. Mention buildings, paths which are shown like this ...., roads, trees and fields.

Checking Your Progress! Working with one or two friends, look carefully at your answers. If your answers are different to theirs look at the map again and try to reach agreement on the answer.

Enclosure maps can also be found for many areas after 1740. These maps were drawn up when open fields and common land were enclosed by hedges. It is possible to tell from numbers on the map who was awarded each piece of land. The common land might still exist in your town or village in the form of allotments which people can rent in order to grow fruit and vegetables.

Let's look at two maps which you discovered in your box and see what we can find out about the area shown.

EXTENSION ACTIVITY

1 Now look at **B**. This is a map of the same area as shown in **A** but the scale of the map is much smaller and so you can see more of the surrounding area. Notice that this is the 1919 edition of the map.
- How many years are there between the map shown in **A** and that shown in **B**?
- What changes have happened in the area between 1894 and 1919? Look at houses, churches, roads and any other changes.
- Now find a friend and compare the changes you have noticed with the ones they have spotted.
- Either draw a diagram or write an explanation about the changes which have happened.

11. BUILDINGS AS EVIDENCE

Target

* To learn how to use buildings as historical evidence.

Station House. The platform side.

? *For whom might this house have been built?*

Buildings are part of our everyday life and most of us are surrounded by many different types. Some may have stood for many, many years, others may be quite modern. However, from the newest to the oldest building, we can learn something from the past.

There are many different uses for buildings. Some might have an official use - like your town hall. Others are places where people live. They may be very grand - like a castle or palace, or they may be the homes of ordinary people.

Over the years the use of a building is often changed. For example a large house might be converted into a home for old people or it might become a shop. Even churches are sometimes converted to other uses. Think of your own house. It may not be very old but you might have had an extension built or new windows put in. All these alterations tell us something about the people who lived there and what happened in the past.

Using some photographs from your box I want to show you how to investigate a building. Have a good look at the photographs shown in this unit before you begin.

CORE ACTIVITIES

In these activities you are going to explore, observe, describe and record information from the site. I hope that you will also begin to ask questions about what you see.

1 Imagine you can walk around the three sides of the building shown in the photographs. Now sit down on the platform looking across the railway lines at Station House.
- Make a careful sketch of the front of the building.
- Try to identify and label each of these features:
  - chimney
  - a sash window
  - a window sill
  - guttering
  - the railway line
  - the platform
- Draw a ground plan showing the house and railway line.

2 Look again at all three photographs.
- Can you find any evidence of alterations or repair work? Draw a sketch to show the alterations using labels to explain what has been changed.
- What questions would you like to ask about this building?
  (*CLUE TO SUCCESS*: Unit 5 might help you with your questions)
- What other evidence might you try to find in order to learn more about the history of the building?
  (*CLUE TO SUCCESS*: Look back at Units 4, 7, 9 and 10)

The front and south side, showing the waiting area.

? *What do you think was built there before the waiting area? (CLUE TO SUCCESS: Look at the brickwork)*

A close up of the platform side.

? *Do you think all parts of this house were built at the same time?*

? *What evidence supports your answers?*

EXTENSION ACTIVITIES

1 Look back at the Core Activities. Using these to help you, you can now look at a real building on site rather than working from photographs.
- Choose a building to look at. It could be your school or your own house. Your teacher will help you choose a building. You might like to take photographs as well as making drawings.

2 Sometimes we do not have enough evidence to be able to put together a complete history of a building. There are two things we can do which might help us to learn a little more.

First, we can look at similar properties to see if the one we are studying is typical of buildings from that time. Nunthorpe Station House was built over 100 years ago.
- Try to find another station house in your area built about 1860.
- Draw sketches or take photographs and compare your building to Nunthorpe Station House.

Second, we can use our own ideas to think about what life might have been like in the house when it was first built. This is called HISTORICAL IMAGINATION.
- Write a short report about life in the house during the 1860s. You could mention heating, lighting, cooking, the occupation of the person or people living there, whether they would be poor or wealthy. (*CLUE TO SUCCESS*: Try to use the photographs in this unit as supporting evidence for your ideas. For example the rooms were probably heated by coal fires as there are chimney pots on the roof)

12. PROBLEMS OF EVIDENCE

Target

* To recognise the problems of historical evidence.
* To identify links and connections between the evidence in Units 1 to 11.

Problem 1: Do we have all the evidence?

In Units 1 to 11 you have been using evidence from your box to build up a picture of the past. Although you have looked at a wide variety of evidence you have to remember that a lot of other useful evidence has been lost or destroyed. So we cannot say that we have a complete picture of the past. It is rather like a jigsaw puzzle with lots of missing pieces. We can only say that this is how things might have been for some people, in a particular place, at a certain time, based upon the evidence which we have available. We cannot say that this is how things were for everyone at that time.

Problem 2: Is the evidence reliable?

When using historical evidence we have to be able to assess its reliability. In other words, can we trust the evidence? There are several questions we need to ask:

- Is the evidence authentic?
- Does it actually come from the time we are studying?
- Was it actually written by the author?

Sometimes the only way to check for authenticity is to compare the evidence to other evidence from the same period.

- Is the evidence biased?

When asking this question we have to decide whether the evidence is one-sided.
Let me give you two examples of evidence being one-sided.

Example 1:
If you were studying the First World War and only looked at photographs as evidence this wouldn't provide a balanced selection of evidence.

Example 2:
If you only read what British soldiers had written about the war and did not look at evidence written by German soldiers, then you would have evidence from only one viewpoint.

To find out if a person has written from a one-sided viewpoint we need to ask the following questions:

Who was the writer?
Why was he or she writing?
Did they hold a particular viewpoint?
How soon after the event was the evidence written?
Did the writer actually see the event or know the person?
Might the writer have had reasons for not telling the truth?

Can we find other evidence which supports the evidence we are using? If we can find evidence written by another person which seems to support the evidence we are studying then this might help us establish that the evidence is reliable.

CORE ACTIVITIES

1 Look back at all the written evidence you have studied in the units so far.
- For each piece of evidence try to decide whether it is reliable by answering the following questions:
  - Is it authentic? How do you know?
  - Is the evidence biased? Explain your answer.
  - Can you find any other evidence to support the evidence you are using? If so, give details.
  (*CLUE TO SUCCESS*: Read this unit again. Remember that you might need to ask other questions)

2 Now let's look at some other evidence.
- Draw up the following chart in your exercise book.

PHOTOGRAPHS	ARTEFACTS	ORAL EVIDENCE	MAPS	BUILDINGS
Example:	Example:	Example:	Example:	Example:
Problems:	Problems:	Problems:	Problems:	Problems:

- Choose one example of each type of evidence.
- Make a list of the problems which you think might be connected with each type of evidence.

EXTENSION ACTIVITY

1 In Unit 1 of this book, you were asked to find out who might be the owner of the box of evidence. You are now going to search for links and connections between all the evidence in Units 1 to 11. Here are some questions and clues to help.

Connection 1: People.
- Can you link together pieces of evidence about the same person or family?
- Write a short history about the person or family, including as much information as possible.
- Make a list of the evidence you have used.
- What further evidence would you try to find?

Connection 2: Places.
- Is it possible to link any of the evidence to particular places?

Connection 3: Events.
- Does the evidence refer to any particular events?
- What can you learn about the events from the evidence?
- What further evidence would you try to find to learn more?

13. THE CONCEPTS OF HISTORY

Target

* To begin to understand the historical concepts of change and continuity, causation and motivation.

Throughout this book you have been learning how to interpret historical evidence. The skills you have learnt are important ones for the study of history. However, you also need to know something about historical concepts.

A concept is not something solid like a table or chair. It is an idea which we carry around in our minds. There are several key ideas or concepts in history and I want to introduce you to these in this unit.

Change

Throughout your study of history you will be looking at how things have changed. You will notice that some changes happen very quickly, while other changes happen very slowly.

A

10 - 14 million years ago.

1.5 million years ago.

42 000 years ago.

The evolution (development) of human beings.

? *Do you think this is an example of very slow or very quick change?*

B

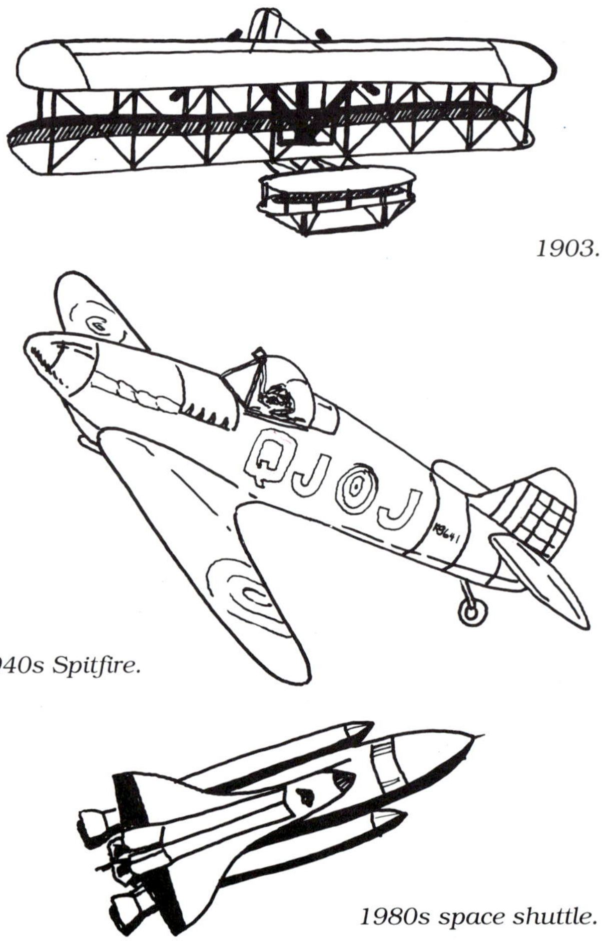

1903.

1940s Spitfire.

1980s space shuttle.

The evolution of flight.

? *Is this is an example of very slow or very quick change? Give reasons for your answer.*

A and **B** also seem to suggest that change means things graduallly getting better. Since the early 1900s aircraft seem to have gradually got bigger and faster. Human beings have even landed on the moon and explored outer space. We could call this sort of change PROGRESS. But change does not always mean that things get better. Some changes mean that things get worse. We call this sort of change REGRESSION.

C

Early 400s A.D. The Romans leave Britain.

Their houses, baths and public buildings begin to crumble.

Other tribes begin to invade Britain.

? *Do you think this is an example of change which leads to progress or change which leads to regresssion? Give reasons for your answer.*

We also know that the same changes happen at different times in different places.

D

3 000 B.C. Cuneiform writing developed in ancient Sumer (modern day Iraq).

2 500 B.C. Hieroglyphic writing developed in ancient Egypt.

? *Why do you think change in the past has often happened in a different time and place?*

Why does change happen?
Change usually happens for a variety of reasons. Historians call these reasons FACTORS. A factor is something which influences change.

An important change during the late 1700s in Britain was that many people moved from the countryside into towns. Let's look at the factors which influenced this change.

Causation

This rather complicated word simply means what CAUSES an event to happen and what EFFECT that event has on people and future events. **F** should help you sort this idea out! Look at **E** first.

E

Factor 1
Changes in farming meant there were fewer jobs in the countryside.

Factor 2
There were jobs available at the new factories being built in towns.

F

CAUSE	EFFECT	THIS CAUSES	EFFECT
1900s population growing	Not enough food	Farmers to develop machinery and better crops	Fewer workers are needed to operate the machinery on farms
EFFECT	**THIS CAUSES**	**EFFECT**	**THIS CAUSES**
Sickness and disease spreads very quickly	People to live in very poor overcrowded conditions	Towns become very overcrowded	People to move to towns in search of work

*Of course there were many other reasons or factors which also influenced these changes but I hope that **F** helps you see how one event can lead to another.*

Motivation

MOTIVATION might be a new word for you. Can you think of a similar word which you might have heard the police use in connection with a crime? I hope you thought of the word motive. This is the word used by the police when they are trying to decide why aperson might have committed a crime. Motivation is a similar word. We use it in history when we are trying to decide what motivated people to behave in a certain way.

Look again at **B** on page 26. Do you remember how quickly flight seemed to have developed? But why did it happen? What motivated people to fly? Let's look at this question more closely.

I have filled in some possible ideas about what motivated people to develop flight.

? *Can you add any further motives?*

Continuity

So far all the ideas or concepts in this unit have been about change. Of course there are things in history which have changed very little. For example the basic ingredients in bread today are very similar to those in bread which was eaten before the time of Christ.

CORE ACTIVTIES

You might find it helps if you work through these activities with a friend.

1 Look back to **A** and **B**.
- Can you think of an example of quick change in your life?
- Can you think of an example of slow change in your life?

2 Look back to **C** and **D**.
- Can you think of a change which has led to progress in our lives today?
- Can you think of a change which has led to regression in our lives today?

3 ● Make a careful copy of **A**. Around your drawings write out the factors which might have influenced the evolution of human beings. (*CLUE TO SUCCESS*: Read the section 'Why does change happen?' on page 28)

4 Look again at **F**, page 28.
- Now draw up your own flow chart of cause and effect about something connected with your own life or life today.
  You could begin with:
  Cause - because I watched television I did not do my homework.
  Effect ?????

5 ● Can you think of an example of continuity in your life today?

EXTENSION ACTIVITY

Using Units 1-12 and any other books available, try to find examples of the following from history:

1 Examples of quick change and slow change.
2 An example of a change which brought about progress. An example which led to regression.
3 An example of causation.
4 An example of continuity.

You could use large sheets of paper to draw and write about your ideas, for other members of the class to see.

14. ORGANISATION/PRESENTATION

Target

* That you should begin to think about the many different ways in which you can organise and present your work.

You have learnt many of the SKILLS you will need to study history and I have introduced you to some of the concepts which will help you understand history. However, you also need to think about the best ways of organising and presenting your work.

ORGANISATION

Your teacher will have been helping you to keep your work organised as you have studied each unit from this book. Remember to set your work out neatly and clearly. Any notes should be made under headings. Often diagrams can present information more clearly than notes. For example have another look at some of the spider diagrams and flow charts you have made as part of the activities in this book.

PRESENTATION

Once you have investigated the past and collected information and evidence together, you need to decide the best way of presenting the results of your investigation. Below are some suggestions for presenting your work which you might like to discuss with other members of your group and your teacher. Some of these suggestions you have already tried out as you worked through this book.

WRITTEN ACCOUNTS

Probably most of your work willl be presented as a piece of writing but this can be done in many ways.

ORAL PRESENTATION

This means a presentation which involves some speaking. For example you could give a talk to the rest of the class on the historical topic you have been studying. Working with some of your friends you could make a radio programme and record it on a cassette. If your school has a video camera you might be able to make a television programme about the topic you have studied. The best way of presenting the information you have collected might be in the form of a play. This is often called a dramatic reconstruction.

A

STORY	PROJECT	NEWSPAPER REPORT
This should explain what happened.	This could include: drawings, diagrams, maps, graphs, photographs. Examples of primary and secondary evidence.	Set your work out like a newspaper. Include drawings or photographs. You could write this as an eye-witness account, but remember you must always use the facts you have learnt from the evidence.

VISUAL PRESENTATION

Perhaps you could display your findings so that other people can come and look. Your work could be displayed on the wall in your classroom or perhaps in the entrance hall of your school. If you decide to present your work in the form of a display make sure that it is colourful and attractive. Make clear abels so that people will understand what the display is about. Use photographs and drawings as well as written naterial. You might even be ıble to set up your own class nuseum using artefacts. Remember you will also need to nclude some written explanation about the evidence ou use.

Dramatic reconstruction of First World War.

COMPUTERS

f you have a computer either at ome or at school then you night be able to use it to help resent your work. You could esign a computer game based n the information you have iscovered when studying a articular topic. Using the omputer as a word processor ou could also type out your eports and accounts.

he important thing is that you hould enjoy studying history. ou could even set up your own istory club!!

Acknowledgements

The author and publishers would like to thank the following for permission to reproduce photographs and other material:

Page	8	B	Syndication International
Page	11	B	The Northern Echo
Page	12	A	Norman Moorsom (reproduced from Vintage Middlesbrough)
Page	20	A	From the 1894 (Sheet XVI. 12) Ordnance Survey map
Page	21	B	From the 1919 (Sheet XVI. S.E.) Ordnance Survey map
Page	27	D	Courtesy of the Trustees of the British Museum

Thanks are also due to:

The British Library (Map Library)
The British Library (Newspaper Library)
Stills Photographic Studios

The author would also like to thank:

Mr J.R. Maddison and the late Mrs O. Maddison
Mr and Mrs M. Brown
The late Mr and Mrs R. Barker
Mrs L. Maddison

Illustrators:

Denby Designs
Jillian Luff of Bitmap Graphics

First published 1990 by Folens Limited.

ISBN 1 85276 106 7

Published by Folens Limited
Dunstable and Dublin

Folens Limited, Albert House, Apex Business Centre, Boscombe Road, Dunstable, LU5 4RL, England.